VICTORI

Commemorati

JUBILEE JEWL

– A GUIDE FOR COLLECTORS –

Pamela M. Caunt

A carte-de-visite of Queen Victoria, dated 1897,
by Rafael Tuck & Sons Ltd, published in commemoration
of the Diamond Jubilee

A young lady in her finery wearing a Golden Jubilee
commemorative brooch made of coins, 1887.

Contents

Introduction

♛

Golden Jubilee 1887

On 21st June, 1887, Victoria, Queen and Empress of lands on which the sun never set, drove from Buckingham Palace to Westminster Abbey to give thanks to God for her fifty years on the Throne of England. Thousands of her subjects from all over the globe, together with her British subjects, lined the richly decorated streets in the hope of catching a glimpse of the Monarch they loved so devotedly. The Press, meanwhile, were loudly acclaiming her achievements during her reign: the railways, free trade and export, the telegraph, progress, prosperity and peace.

Queen Victoria initially had not been a willing participant in the Golden Jubilee celebrations and it was only after much persuading that she agreed to end her twenty-six years of almost total seclusion after the death of Albert, her Consort.

Although Royal events had been celebrated for hundreds of years, the Golden Jubilee was the first ever to be recorded. In order to mark the occasion Queen Victoria had to relax her rule of deep mourning and, as a result, there came about a huge demand for commemorative jewellery of all types, including badges, brooches, bracelets, lockets, pendants and chains. So great was it, that manufacturers were caught unawares as demand far exceeded supply, prompting 'The Watchmaker, Jeweller and Silversmith' magazine to declare that, 'it was a pity Jubilees came around so seldom . . . .'.

Numerous official medals, issued by the Crown, were struck to commemorate the Golden Jubilee. The gentlemen of the Freemasons had their own especially designed for them and hundreds of thousands of souvenir medals were issued to hand out free to schoolchildren or, for a small charge, to members of various societies and associations.

The market for the cheaper type of commemorative jewellery was aimed at the 'clerks' classes'. Women in this group were now working, and keeping their own money, for the first time. This bought with it a new-found independence and the ability to purchase their own jewellery. The ladies of the middle and upper classes would purchase the more expensive silver and gold pieces, some of which would have been set with diamonds and other precious stones.

The design of Jubilee jewellery relied heavily on the application of motifs, monograms and dates. Brooches and pins were the most common types but as padlock bracelets and watch chains grew in popularity, so did charms which could easily be attached. Coins, dated 1887, mounted as brooches or set behind glass to form a fob or pendant, became another craze for the fashion conscious. Jet continued to be worn by those in mourning and even this austere substance was given the Jubilee treatment (see p. 21).

Months before the June festivities began, customers were flocking to view the over-filled windows of the classiest shops in London's Bond Street and Regent Street. In other areas, stalls displayed cheaper versions of the same designs and the street hawkers' trays were piled high with beribboned, paper rosettes and cheap medals.

Whilst this mass-produced jewellery was being bought by her subjects, Queen Victoria, a huge bestower of commemorative gifts, was presenting pierced gold brooches, set with diamonds, to the princesses just prior to the Jubilee banquet. At the back there was a glass box containing a photograph of the Queen. To the princes and favourite male members of her Household, she gave gold stick pins also set with diamonds. The youngest members of her family received commemorative trifles no doubt including the Jubilee trumpet brooches with enamelled banners which she had commissioned from Garrards, the Crown Jewellers. A considerable amount of commemorative jewellery was also received by the Queen from her very large family here and on the Continent. The most famous piece is the 'Jubilee necklace' (see p. 44) which consists of diamond trefoils set with pearls. This was presented to her by the 'Women of the British Empire' and bought with the residue of money subscribed for the Albert Memorial in Hyde Park.

Diamond Jubilee 1897

During the ten years following her Golden Jubilee, Queen Victoria never again reverted to her former seclusion and her popularity grew and grew. The long time she had spent on the Throne was seen as sixty glorious years of peace. Sixty years in which England had amassed a wealth of riches and accumulated a vast dominion. It is not surprising that the Diamond Jubilee was even more grandiose than the Golden Jubilee and every town, village and hamlet came out to celebrate. In London, once again, thousands thronged the richly decorated thoroughfares. The grand procession took a much wider berth than before and its numbers were swelled enormously as every Colony had sent out a detachment of troops. Wave after wave of Maoris, Jamaicans, Nigerians, Canadians, South Africans, Australians and Indians accompanied the Queen's carriage, drawn by eight cream-coloured horses, from Buckingham Palace to St. Paul's Cathedral.

Jewellery manufacturers, endeavouring to learn from their mistakes in 1887, decided that this time the supply of commemorative trinkets would not run out. It became boom time once again and the many industrial strikes which were concurrently taking place around the country did little to mar the makers' success. Official medals were issued once again and another huge output of souvenir medals was struck.

Many of the designs for Diamond Jubilee jewellery were similar in idea to those of the Golden Jubilee, however, others were more adventurous such as the 'Unionist Lorgnette

Chain' which was made up of alternate rubies, diamonds and sapphires to represent the red, white and blue, and the gold lockets shaped out of sovereigns containing a photograph of the Queen. Cuff links, now a new fashion accessory superceding the 'solitaires' or 'batchelors buttons' previously worn, and now referred to as 'sleeve links', particularly lent themselves to commemorative jewellery in that paired heads (young and old), and paired dates (1837 and 1897), could be used. Mappin and Webb sold silver buckles for ladies' waistbands embodying the same motifs (see p. 20). Pocket watches were also transformed into Jubilee souvenirs with miniature profiles of the Queen applied to the cases.

A general skimpiness, however, had now crept into mass-produced Jubilee jewellery. Pieces were smaller, thinner metal was used and less enamel was applied. Competition began to come in from America where, in Newark, New Jersey, tin button badges were manufactured carrying either photographs of the Queen or other Royal emblems.

As during the Golden Jubilee, Queen Victoria was once again handing out trinkets to her children and grandchildren and, once again, hordes of jewels streamed in from all over the world. One of the most famous pieces was the 'Jubilee Brooch', (see p. 45) which was presented to the Queen by members of her Household.

Collecting

Royal commemorative jewellery has always been popular throughout the various stratas of society but never more so than at the time of Victoria's two Jubilees. Interest in collecting it has now been revived both in England and in America and it is therefore becoming increasingly difficult to find. Antique stalls are the most obvious place to look but antique shops and galleries are also worth a try. Collectors hoping to see Jubilee jewellery amassed together will be disappointed. Very few Museums rate it highly enough to hold collections, however, the Museum of London does have some 'below stairs' and other examples may be found in Cheltenham, Birmingham and the Victoria and Albert Museums.

In order to learn a little more about this type of jewellery, collectors must first of all look at the methods of manufacture. In the main, mass-produced Jubilee jewellery, and not that given to or by the Queen herself, was manufactured in Birmingham although some was made in London, Chester and Sheffield. The introduction of more advanced machinery at the turn of the eighteenth century had turned jewellery making into a huge industry and ten times more pieces could now be made than when produced by hand.

The main machine used in production was the 'drop stamp machine' which consisted of two parts, the 'die' and the 'force'. The 'die sinker' was regarded as the key craftsman and was responsible for cutting and chiselling the original design into the 'die'. The 'force', which corresponded in shape to the sunken impression of the 'die', rose and fell like a guillotine at the kick of an operator's foot, forcing small metal discs on to the 'die', so taking on the desired shape. This would then be neatened and the required motifs and beads soldered on by hand. Final touches of engraving and sections of enamel were added later by 'outdoor workers' who set up small workshops in the vicinity of the factories. The fixings and finishing would also be done by 'outdoor workers' as would the carding and boxing.

Medals were also stamped out using the above method but the cheaper ribbon rosettes and cardboard badges would have been made by hand by whole families working from home. Even the smallest children had to contribute in some way, and for little or no reward.

When trying to decide whether or not to purchase a piece of jewellery, collectors should closely examine the article. If it is a brooch, replacement pins and hooks can clearly be identified by the small plate needed to mount new fixings and new pins are invariably shorter as Victorian ladies liked to tuck the extended part into the folds of their dress to make it more secure as safety catches had not yet been invented. Locket-back brooches often have the glass as well as the bezel, the rim around it, missing. Hollow jewellery is often dented and this is almost impossible to repair. Lockets often refuse to close or have splits along the edges – these can be repaired. Lead solder, showing that a piece has been badly repaired, is a jeweller's nightmare as it cannot be removed and has often etched its way into the article. Medals are usually found to be in relatively good condition being more robust and obviously not worn so often.

It is almost impossible to put an exact value on Jubilee jewellery as so much depends on condition, rarity and, most importantly, on how much the buyer is prepared to pay. However, approximate values have been given in this book but should merely be used as a rough, general guide.

To conclude, the commemorative Jubilee jewellery included in this book, with the exception of the two pieces from the Royal Collection, has all been mass-produced. It was probably worn for a short while only and then put away, in a drawer, to be finally unearthed as a family treasure. In this way it offers us a clear insight, not only into the mood of the moment, but also into the fashions and foibles of the people who wore it. It also serves to illustrate how Victorians loved to commemorate events of all kinds by adorning themselves with the relevant trinkets. These could record great tragedies, favourite pastimes, or loyal allegiances. Jubilee jewellery particularly shows us, one hundred years later, the Victorians' fidelity to the Throne and their devotion to their revered Queen – sentiments which are fast disappearing in today's world.

Pamela M. Caunt
London
1997

PLATE I
Coloured Enamel and Silver Brooches
Golden Jubilee

PLATE II
Silver Brooches
Golden Jubilee

PLATE I

Coloured Enamel and Silver Brooches
Golden Jubilee

Approximate value £35 – £55

1. An oblong brooch with beaded edge, enamelled Royal Standard, applied crown and letters 'VR', and engraved patriotic motifs. R.J.W., Birm.
2. A hollow buckled strap brooch with an enamelled border inscribed 'Victoria Regina 1837–1887' enclosing enamelled crossed flags and crown. Unmarked.
3. An oblong brooch with beaded edge and enamelled buckled strap centre-piece, with crossed flags and crown, pinned through, and crossed flags applied either side. Unmarked.
4. A horseshoe brooch with a beaded edge and enamelled Royal Standard and crown pinned through. The word 'Jubilee', 'VR' and crossed flags have been applied and '1837 – 1887' has been inscribed. B. Bros, Birm.
5. A stamped out brooch in the shape of a laurel wreath with a crossed mace and sceptre and enamelled Royal Standard surmounted by a crown pinned through and applied letters 'VR' either side. S. Bros, Birm.
6. A horseshoe brooch with beaded edge and enamelled crown pinned through. The letters 'VR' and a spray of patriotic motifs have been applied. Unmarked.
7. An oval brooch with beaded edge and enamelled Royal Standard with crossed sceptre and mace surmounted by a crown, pinned through. Applied patriotic motifs curl along the left-hand side and it is inscribed '1837–1887'. K & M, Birm.
8. A red and blue enamelled shield with laurel wreath has been pinned through to a crossed sceptre and mace. Reg. no. 60869.
9. An oval buckled strap brooch with beaded edge, inscribed '37 Jubilee 87'. An enamelled Royal Standard, with crossed sceptre and mace surmounted by a crown, has been pinned through. The letters 'VR' have been applied either side and there is a locket at the back. Unmarked.
10. A brooch, stamped out in two pieces, enclosing a locket-back with a laurel wreath and bow applied to the front. An enamelled Royal Standard, surmounted by a crown has been pinned through. S. Bros, Birm.
11. A crescent shaped brooch stamped out in two pieces, the beaded edge being an integral part. The enamelled letters 'VR', surmounted by a crown, have been pinned through. Unmarked.
12. An oval brooch with a scalloped edge inscribed 'Jubilee 1837–1887'. A profile of Queen Victoria has been applied to the enamelled Royal Standard and the whole motif pinned through. The letters 'VR' have been applied and there is a locket at the back. Unmarked.
13. A hollow crescent brooch with a beaded edge with blue enamelled '37 Jubilee 87'. The enamelled Royal Standard, surmounted by a crown, has been pinned through. Unmarked.
14. A shield shaped brooch, surmounted by a crown, with a beaded edge. The blue enamelled buckled strap motif has been pinned through and the corners tipped with gold. Unmarked.
15. A similar brooch to (13) but with a gilded crown and patriotic motifs pinned through. Unmarked.
16. Crossed hollow sceptres form the basis of this brooch on to which an enamelled Royal Standard has been applied. Unmarked.
17. A blue enamelled hollow buckled strap bears the word 'Jubilee' and the dates '1837 and 1887'. The enamelled flag has been soldered to the front. W.J.D., Birm.
18. A hollow lion strides across the Royal mace. The enamelled Royal Standard has been soldered on. Unmarked.
19. Enamelled red, white and blue Royal Standards, surmounted by crowns with a riband beneath, have all been stamped out in one piece. A second flat piece has been soldered to the back forming a hollow brooch. Unmarked.
20. A tiny, hollow heart inscribed 'Victoria 37 87 Jubilee' has an enamelled Royal Standard with crossed sceptres and crown, pinned through. Unmarked.
21. An oval gilded brooch stamped out in two sections has an integral beaded edge and a locket-back. Enamelled Irish and English flags, surmounted by a crown, and applied with a padlock, have been pinned through. the riband reads '1837 Jubilee 1887'. Unmarked.

Private collection.

PLATE II
Silver Brooches
Golden Jubilee
Approximate value £25 – £40

1. A very complex brooch which has been cast rather than stamped out. It incorporates the letters 'VR', 'EI', for Empress of India, the Royal Standard, patriotic motifs, the words, 'In commemoration of the Jubilee of our beloved Queen's prosperous reign' and the dates '1837 and 1886/7'. I.A., Chester.
2. A shield-shaped brooch with beaded top and applied laurel wreath, Union Jack, 'VR' and '1887'. The word 'Jubilee' has been inscribed on the riband at the bottom. H & N, Chester.
3. A hollow horseshoe brooch with blue enamelled inscription '1837 Victoria Jubilee 1887' and the shield, crown and patriotic motifs pinned through. The horseshoe at this time always pointed downwards. It was only during the First World War that it was reverted to prevent the 'luck running out'. Unmarked.
4. A circular brooch, stamped out in two pieces incorporating a locket-back. The crown and the word 'Jubilee' have been applied and the patriotic emblems have been engraved. R.J.W., Birm.
5. A hollow brooch stamped out in two pieces which is a good example of the die-sinker's art as the Queen's head, buckled strap, lettering and flags are all shown in great detail. J.W.T., Birm. Reg. no. 60350.
6. A hollow horseshoe brooch has had a flat plate soldered to the front and the head of Victoria applied. The word 'Jubilee' has also been applied as have the beads around the edge. K & M, Birm.
7. This oblong brooch has strip cartouche applied decoration, applied 'Jubilee' and engraved dates '1837 and 1887', together with engraved patriotic emblems. W.G., Birm.
8. A locket-back brooch with applied crown and patriotic motifs enhanced with engraved foliage. R.J.W., Birm.
9. The crown, letters 'VR' and patriotic emblems have all been stamped out together with the front of this oval brooch illustrating another good example of the die-sinker's art. It has a beaded edge and a locket-back. J.W.T., Birm.
10. A circular, beaded edge brooch which has been enhanced with a pierced, gold-front, motif of a laurel wreath, riband, shield and crown with delicate engraving. H & N, Chester.
11. A hollow brooch showing a bannered trumpet surmounted by a crown with the word 'Victoria' and the dates '1837 and 1887'. This may well have been inspired by the Garrard brooches which the Queen commissioned as Jubilee souvenirs for the youngest members of her family. F.V., Birm. Reg. no. 60945.
12. A hollow mace has a riband wrapped around and soldered to it to form this very pretty brooch. 'Guard our Queen', the Royal Standard and 'VR' have all been engraved and the patriotic emblems at the top have been cut out. Unmarked.
13. A quatrefoil brooch of crowns stamped out in two sections with an applied profile of the Queen. T & Co., Birm. Reg. no. 60844.
14. Two hollow maces form the basis of a brooch which has a crystal intaglio set into the centre into which is cut Victoria's Imperial crown. Birm. Reg. no. 60618.
15. An enormous amount of detail has been stamped into this brooch including integral beads, twisted ropework, a finely executed Royal Standard and intricate crowns. Laurels are applied at the bottom. M & J, Birm.
16. A circular brooch very similar in design to (10) but much smaller. Unmarked.

Private collection.

PLATE III

Coloured Enamel and Silver Brooches
Diamond Jubilee

PLATE IV
Gold Jewellery
Golden and Diamond Jubilees

PLATE III
Coloured Enamel and Silver Brooches
Diamond Jubilee
Approximate value £25 — £40

1. A gilded brooch with the dates '1837 – 97' engraved on the cross-bar with a crossed flag and crown motif applied to the front. The anchor was a very popular design in Victorian times not only for its naval connection but it was also the symbol for 'hope'. S. Bros, Birm.
2. A simple date brooch was struck in an attempt to imitate marcasite or paste-set jewellery which was fashionable at the time. C & N, Birm.
3. Another date brooch incorporating a wish-bone, or 'merrythought' as it was called in Victorian times. C & N, Birm.
4. A simple brooch enamelled in two colours with an integral beaded edge. The dates '1837 and 1897' are either side of the letter. 'V'. G.L., Birm.
5. A beaded edge brooch with diaper engraving behind the words 'Victoria' and 'Jubilee'. An enamelled Royal Standard has been pinned through and a profile of Victoria applied. Patriotic emblems are engraved at the top and bottom. Unmarked.
6. A solid brooch which has been cast rather than stamped out. The central disc containing Victoria's profile has been pinned through and the letters 'VR' have been enamelled in blue. A spray of roses forms the background. J.F., Chester. Reg. no. 283576.
7. A tiny hollow double-heart brooch with an intengral beaded edge. The words 'the longest reign' and the profile of the Queen were stamped out and the dates '1837 – 1897' have been engraved. R.J.W., Birm. Reg. no. 195838.
8. A shielded-shaped, enamelled, Royal Standard, surmounted by a crown, is enhanced by the addition of pastes set into cup-shaped collets containing gold foil for brighter sparkle. GL & Co., Birm.
9. A pierced brooch the design of which consists of crossed flags, 'VR' and patriotic emblems all set into a hollow border. WT & S, Birm.
10. Similar in design to (8) but set onto a bar bearing the dates '1837 and 1897' with a bead at each end. GL & Co, Birm.
11. Similar in concept to no. (2). C & N, Birm.
12. A hollow brooch with a beaded edge has the profile of Victoria pinned through. Two different coloured golds have been applied to the surface. WL, Birm.
13. A hollow brooch again with the profile of Queen Victoria and the use of two different coloured golds. PP & Co, Birm.
14. A hollow brooch with applied dates and crown. ALLE, Birm.
15. A cast brooch incorporating 'VRI' for Victoria Regina and India, the dates '1837 to 1897', and the word 'sexagenary'. Shamrocks, thistles and bows further enhance the design. IMS. Reg. no. 286005.
16. Diamond Jubilee brooches became much skimpier than those made for the Golden Jubilee. A good example is this brooch which is of little substance and has a laurel wreath motif and dates applied to the front. P & T, Birm.
17. A dainty brooch with applied letters 'VR', crown, dates and patriotic emblems. S. Bros, Birm.
18. A crossed mace and sceptre form the background for young and old heads of Victoria. 'Long has she reigned' has been stamped out on the riband at the bottom. A crown on a Bible surmount the brooch and the monogram 'VR' is in the centre of the lower edge. T. Bros, Chester.
19. A hollow, scalloped, crescent provides the base for this pretty brooch. The encircled head of the Queen, the patriotic emblems and the dates have all been carefully cut out and applied. R.J.W., Birm.

Private collection.

These Diamond Jubilee brooches, together with those on the previous two colour plates, would all have been stamped out using the 'drop stamp machine', with the exception of the cast pieces. The hollow beads around the edges would have been soldered on individually by hand.

PLATE IV
Gold Jewellery
Golden and Diamond Jubilees
Approximate value £30 – £85

1. A brown enamelled portrait of the Queen at the time of her accession to the Throne, mounted in a gold surround. The reverse shows a portrait of the Queen at the time of her Diamond Jubilee.

2. A blue enamelled portrait of the Queen at the time of her Diamond Jubilee reversing to a 'young head'. It is a smaller version of the above and again mounted in gold.

3. A gold crown decorated with garnets and paste surmounts the Royal monogram set with pearls on this pretty brooch. There is a riband at the lower edge engraved with the dates '1837 and 1887' and patriotic emblems are applied to each end.

Numbers (1) and (2) private collection, number (3) courtesy of Les Stevens.

Gold Jubilee jewellery does not seem to be as plentiful as silver, maybe because people were reluctant to invest larger sums of money in something that would be worn for a short time only. Many of the trade advertisements at the time, however, suggest that each design illustrated could be ordered in either base metal, silver or gold. Charms and pendants were extremely fashionable for the Diamond Jubilee, none more so than the above enamelled portraits of the Queen. To make these, a photograph would be placed on a copper medallion which had been prepared to receive it by having a surface of enamel applied. The article was then placed on a sheet of metal and fired in a furnace. As soon as the piece was taken from the furnace, the enamel would set. The portraits would then either be mounted in gold or silver. Rubies, emeralds and pearls were used extensively in gold Jubilee jewellery to represent the rose, the shamrock and the thistle. The leek was not included at this time as Wales was not yet a principality. The date '1897' was popular made in gold, and for a price of £4 4s. 0d. the brooch could be set with twenty-three diamonds and one whole pearl.

PLATE V
Lockets, Fobs and Charms
Golden and Diamond Jubilees

PLATE VI

Silver Coin Jewellery
Golden Jubilee

PLATE V
Lockets, Fobs and Charms
Golden and Diamond Jubilees
Approximate value £5 — £40

1. A photograph of Queen Victoria set within a silver, glass-sided, fob with beaded edge is surmounted by a silver lion. A halfpenny stamp is set into the reverse. C^E & P, Chester, 1897.

2. An enamlled silver sixpence mounted in a silver frame, Unmarked, 1887.

3. A silver-gilt, heart-shaped charm with the head of Queen Victoria, a rose, a thistle and shamrocks, surmouned by a crown. JR, Sheffield, 1886.

4. A silver charm bearing profiles of Victoria and her eight children on one side, and twenty-one portraits of other leading members of the Royal family on the other. It is still attached to its original ribbon. Unmarked, 1897.

5. A shilling mounted as a silver watch fob, swivels to show the reverse. L. Bros, Birm., 1886.

6. A silver charm showing the reverse side of no. (4) is suspended from a blue enamel bow. Unmarked, 1897.

7. A square, scalloped edge silver charm with applied gold-fronted letters 'VR' and 'Jubilee' surmounted by a crown. R. Bs., Birm., 1897

8. A small silver charm which would have be stamped out in a single piece. Unmarked, 1897.

9. A silver-gilt locket with letters 'VR' applied, delicate engraving in the corners, and a silver crown on top. Unmarked.

10. A small, oblong silver locket with an applied motif consisting of the letters 'VR', and patriotic emblems with the word 'Jubilee' on a riband. J.C., Birm., 1896.

11. A silver threepenny piece, gilded and set into a bead-edge fob with applied twisted ropework wires. C.E., Birm., 1889.

12. A photograph of the young head of Victoria set into a crystal, brass edged fob reverses to an old head. Unmarked.

13. A photograph of the old head of Victoria set into a heart-shaped crystal, brass edged fob reverses to a young head, Unmarked.

Private collection.

Thousands of these small mementoes were manufactured for both Jubilees either to hang on a neck chain, watch chain or charm bracelet. They were made in all materials from gold to base metal. Some showed the Queen's signature picked out in enamel, others had pearly crowns or hand painted portraits of her Majesty. For the Diamond Jubilee real stones such as moonstones, coral or turquoise, were set into silver threepenny pieces or farthings to add to the glitter of a charm bracelet. The Queen's message to the Nation on her Diamond Jubilee was also interpreted on a tiny charm and reads, 'From my heart, I thank my beloved people, God bless them, Victoria, R. et I., June 22nd, 1897'.

PLATE VI

Silver Coin Jewellery
Golden Jubilee

Approximate value £10 – £40

1. A 'veiled head' silver threepence set into a shield-shaped hollow brooch with integral beaded edge. The letters 'VR' have been applied to the top corners and the word 'Jubilee' is engraved at the bottom. The brooch is surmounted by a silver crown. R. & Co., Birm.
2. A 'Jubilee head' shilling set into a cog-wheel, beaded, mount with swivel action. Unmarked.
3. Five gilded miniature sovereigns soldered together to form a quatrefoil brooch with a simple pin and hook fixings. Unmarked.
4. A 'Jubilee head' sixpence set into a circular, beaded mount. Unmarked.
5. A silver arrow brooch with three 'Jubilee head' threepences soldered to it, one showing the reverse, and two the obverse. Unmarked.
6. Two silver sixpences soldered together to form a small brooch. The left-hand coin shows the reverse and is enamelled. Unmarked.
7. An enamelled double-florin set into a scrolled, engraved, border with four beads. It has a swivel action set into the top and bottom bead. The double-florin was introduced in 1887 as a step towards the decimalisation of the currency. Equal to two florins or four shillings, the double-florins were unpopular because they were easily confused with five-shilling pieces, crowns. They were discontinued in 1890. Unmarked.
8. An enamelled, gilded, shilling set into a cog-wheel, beaded, mount. Two wires at the back enable the coin to be taken out and reversed to show a gilded 'Jubilee head'. R & Co., Chester.
9. An enamelled sixpence set into a cog-wheel, beaded, mount. A strip and hook device at the back enables the coin to be taken out and reversed. ? T., Birm.
10. An enamelled shilling with a simple pin and hook soldered to the back. Unmarked.
11. An enamelled sixpence set into a glass-fronted, scalloped silver mount. Unmarked.
12. An Indian two-Anna piece has been applied on to crossed, enamelled, flags surmounted by a red crown, and the dates 1837 and 1887. Patriotic emblems in pierced work form a garland along the bottom. Reg. no. 67180.
13. An enamelled sixpence and two plain threepences have been soldered together to form a brooch with a simple pin and hook attached to the back. Unmarked.
14. The reverse sides of two shilling pieces have been soldered together to form a plain brooch with a simple pin and hook attached. Unmarked.
15. A gilded and enamelled half-crown with a simple pin and hook attached. Unmarked.

Private collection.

1887 highlighted the ever-growing fashion of mounting coins to be worn as jewellery. Coins were minted in that year bearing the young head of Queen Victoria wearing her small Imperial crown. This was known as the 'Jubilee head' (see photograph on page 1). Some coins were set into a mount with individual 'beads' soldered around the edge, others had prettily engraved mounts, and the plainest ones merely had a pin and hook soldered to the back. The mount sometimes permitted the wearer to display a choice of either obverse or reverse as the coin would be mounted in such a way that it could swivel around. Enamelling greatly enhanced many of the coins and to achieve this the coins had to be first of all filed and then cleaned with acid. The enamel was made by crushing a special kind of glass oxide, together with water, in a mortar until it resembled sand. This mixture would then be applied and the coin heated in a furnace until it fused. This was done three times and then the coin was stone ground to make sure the surface was even. It was then cleaned once again and refired ready for polishing. When two or more colours were used, the colours not being worked had to be masked for protection. Although the Royal Mint discouraged the use of coins in this way, as it was not the purpose for which they were originally intended, they did not actually carry out the full force of the Law and prosecute offending manufacturers. This disapproval did mean, however, that nowadays little can be learned of this trade and there are no advertisements illustrating such jewellery in trade magazines. Various denominations of coins were used but the shilling, sixpence and threepenny bit were the most popular. Coins of the Commonwealth were also used, see no. (12) above, and watch chains, bracelets and stick pins were also fashioned out of coins. It was a trend that was short-lived, however, and, apart from gold sovereign lockets, far fewer pieces were made for the Diamond Jubilee ten years later.

PLATE VII
Silver Brooches with matching Earrings
Golden Jubilee

PLATE VIII
Silver Buckle
Diamond Jubilee

PLATE IX
Jet Jewellery and its Imitations – Brooches
Golden and Diamond Jubilees

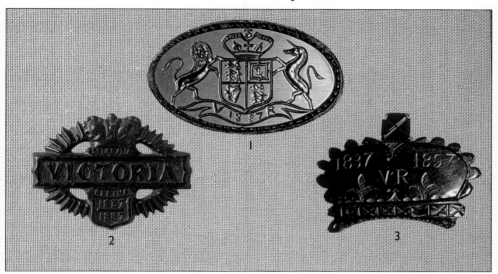

PLATE X
Jet Jewellery and its Imitations – Vulcanite Bangle
Diamond Jubilee

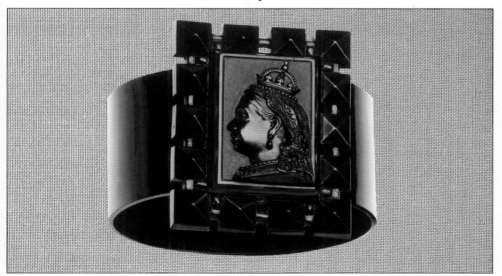

PLATE VII

Silver Brooches with matching Earrings
Golden Jubilee

Approximate value £50 – £90

1. A hollow, star-shaped silver brooch with an integral beaded edge. A blue enamelled buckled strap encircles a silver crown which has been pinned through. The buckle strap was used extensively in 'novelty' jewellery and its influence came from Queen Victoria as she was the Head of the Order of the Garter. The dates '1837 and 1887', together with the words 'Victoria Jubilee', have been left exposed in the enamel. The brooch has a locket-back enabling a photograph or hair to be inserted. The earrings are miniature versions of the brooch and are also hollow with a crown pinned through. Unmarked.

2. A silver, engraved, mace with a crescent soldered to it forms this brooch. A laurel wreath and a riband with the word 'Jubilee' engraved, have been applied to the crescent. In the centre, two shields bearing the applied letters 'VR' and the date '1887' are surmounted by patriotic emblems in pierced work. The earrings are miniature versions of the crescent, enclosing one shield, each bearing an applied letter, 'V' and 'R'. Unmarked.

Private collection.

Matching sets of brooches and earrings were very popular during the 1880s. In fact, a whole parure of 'novelty' jewellery would often include a bracelet, locket and necklet as well. Earrings were coming back into popularity after the 19th century versions which were so heavy that, in addition to a hook through the ear, the wearer would pass a thread over her head, beneath her hair, to lighten the weight on her ear lobes. The designs around the time of the Golden Jubilee were much lighter, smaller and daintier.

PLATE VIII

Silver Buckle
Diamond Jubilee

Approximate value £80 – £100

The young and old heads of Queen Victoria are displayed between the dates 1837 and 1897 respectively on this pierced-work silver buckle. It would be worn on the waistband of a lady's dress with an attached fabric belt. CF ☆ FS, Chester, 1896.

Private collection.

Silver buckles such as the one illustrated were advertised as 'Jubilee Novelties' in popular ladies' magazines such as 'The Queen, the Lady's Newspaper'. They were bought as gifts or souvenirs from such stores as Mappin & Webb in London.

PLATE IX

Jet Jewellery and its Imitations – Brooches
Golden and Diamond Jubilees

Approximate value £25 – £50

1. A typical Whitby jet oval brooch into which the Royal Standard has been carved, 1887.

2. An oval brooch made of pressed horn with 'Victoria Regina' and the dates '1837' and '1887' in relief.

3. A jet brooch in the shape of a crown into which the dates '1887' and '1897', the letters 'VR' and a criss-cross pattern have been carved.

Numbers (1) and (3) courtesy of Helen Muller, number (2) courtesy of Allison Massey.

Jet, a hard lustrous form of natural carbon, was used extensively to make jewellery during the Victorian era and reached the height of fashion in the 1870s. In England it was mainly found in North Yorkshire, the main industry being centred in Whitby. Its popularity first of all stemmed from its lightness in weight in sharp contrast to the heavy pieces worn previously. Secondly, the Queen was in permanent mourning for Albert and had instructed her Court to also wear black for an extended period of time. If black jewellery was required at Court, then the people too elected to wear black jewellery and so the fashion grew. In order for the poorer people to keep up with modern trends the manufacturers devised cheap imitations which included, vulcanite, bog oak, pressed horn and French jet, which is glass. Vulcanite, which was rubber treated with sulphur or sulphur compounds to make it hard, looked very similar to jet as it could be polished to a high sheen. However, exposed to the light, it would fade to a brownish colour. So would bog oak, which was a fossilised wood found in Ireland. Pressed horn could not really be confused with jet as it had a rough look about it especially on the reverse.

PLATE X

Jet Jewellery and its Imitations – Vulcanite Bangle
Diamond Jubilee

Approximate value £95

A vulcanite bangle with the carved profile of Queen Victoria highly polished. Squares surround the central motif and the rest of the bangle is left plain.

Courtesy of Allison Massey.

Vulcanite jewellery, made from rubber, was moulded into shape and then so highly polished that it was hard to distinguish from real jet. Bangles such as the one illustrated, would have been made together with a brooch and they would be worn as a matching set.

PLATE XI
Souvenir Brooch – Railways
Diamond Jubilee

PLATE XII
Souvenir Brooch – Tourism
Diamond Jubilee

PLATE XIII

Base Metal Jewellery
Gold and Diamond Jubilees

PLATE XI
Souvenir Brooch – Railways
Diamond Jubilee
Approximate value £30

An oval silver brooch with beaded edge and applied decorative border. In the centre is an engraving of the Queen Empress locomotive with the name and number, 2054, also engraved. J.W.T., Birm, 1896.

Private collection.

England's railway system became one of the most important factors in the prosperity which endured during Queen Victoria's long reign and when the locomotive, 'Queen Empress', was sent to an exhibition in Chicago as a piece of publicity for Britain and the North Western Railway in 1897, during the Queen's Diamond Jubilee year, it had the whole-hearted support of the British public. The livery of the train was painted a creamy white and apparently, 'never had a locomotive looked so magnificent'. Her sister locomotive, 'Greater Britain', was painted red and it was proposed to paint a third one blue, but this plan never came to fruition. The 'Queen Empress' stands as a good example of how diverse the Birmingham manufacturers were prepared to be in finding themes for Jubilee jewellery. It also shows how women were prepared to wear something as masculine as a brooch embellished with a train on their lacey, high-necked blouses, in order to keep up with current fashion.

PLATE XII
Souvenir Brooch – Tourism
Diamond Jubilee
Approximate value £25

A hollow crescent forms the base of this brooch and the enamelled Royal Standard, crossed maces, date letters and riband inscribed 'Wookey Hole' have been applied later. A.L.L.E., Birm, 1896.

Private collection.

The advent of the railways in Victorian times made travelling much easier and more and people were able to participate in this form of transport thus indulging in the growing trend of 'tourism'. The Birmingham manufacturers saw an opportunity here to devise ranges of 'novelty' jewellery depicting famous buildings, exhibitions, bridges, monuments and even disasters such as the Albion Colliery where two hundred and ninety men and boys were killed – all places to which tourists flocked. 1897 gave them an opportunity to add Jubilee commemorative emblems to their tourist jewellery making it even more desirable. The brooch photographed here would have been bought as a souvenir from Wookey Hole, a beauty spot in Somerset, famous for its caves.

PLATE XIII
Base Metal Jewellery
Golden and Diamond Jubilees
Approximate value £5 – £15

1. A brass star, containing a sepia photograph of Victoria, suspended from a brass bow with pin. The inscription on the reverse reads, 'In commemoration of the 60th year of the reign of Her Majesty Queen Victoria 1897'. Unmarked.

2. A brass laurel wreath brooch with the enamelled Royal Standard in the centre, and surmounted by a crown. The word 'Jubilee' and the dates '1837' and '1887' have been stamped out in one piece with the front. There is a flat back section soldered on. Unmarked.

3. A beaded edge Royal Standard enamelled in four colours with the dates '1837 and 1887' and the word 'Jubilee' across the centre. Unmarked.

4. Yachting jewellery or flag jewellery was 'all the rage' in 1897 and so the manufacturers adapted it to form Jubilee jewellery. They were made from half an inch to nearly two inches long and ranged from base metal to silver gilt and gold. This blue enamel brooch has a red enamelled crown and the letters 'VR' and the dates '1837 – 1897' left exposed in gilt. Unmarked.

5. A large gilt pendant brooch with a faded photograph of the four generations. These include Victoria, the Prince of Wales (King Edward VII), the Duke of York and little Prince Edward of York. The reverse reads, 'To commemorate the Diamond Jubilee of the reign of Queen Victoria 1837 – 1897'. Unmarked.

6. A small enamelled gilt brooch with the enamelled Royal Standard and the letters 'VR' enamelled in blue each side. Unmarked.

7. A circular base metal brooch with enamelled Royal Standard and 'Jubilee' and the dates '1837 and 1887' displayed at the bottom. Unmarked.

8. Three blue enamelled crowns surround a white enamelled 'V' with a red riband underneath denoting 'the longest reign'. Unmarked. (See advertisement on page 43.)

9. A tin stick pin wih a celluloid type photograph of Queen Victoria overprinted with 'Diamond Jubilee' and '1837 and 1897'. The reverse is marked 'Patent approved for City Button Works, Newark, USA'.

10. A simple brass bar brooch with a gold front and integral beaded edge. A silver crown has been soldered to the centre and the dates '1837 and 1897' engraved either side. Unmarked.

11. A circular gilt brooch containing a miniature hand painted portrait of the Queen set in brilliants. Unmarked.

12. A simple brass 'safety pin' with a gold-fronted profile of Victoria and the dates '1837 and 1897' applied. Brilliants are set into the brass riband below. Unmarked. (See advertisement on page 43.)

13. The Watchmaker, Jeweller and Silversmith, April, 1897, described these cufflinks as '*a unique set of commemoration links with real photographs of the Queen on each link. On one button appears the latest portrait of the Queen, and on the other a pretty little miniature as she appeared on her accession to the Throne*'. Marked 'Improved "CSOEZI' patent 13001'.

Private collection.

Base metal Jubilee jewellery was stamped out using the 'drop stamp machine' as described on p. 6. This cheaper type of jewellery relied heavily on enamelling and for this process, see p. 19. Photographs of the Royal family, and especially Victoria, were used in profusion as were the usual motifs of the Royal Standard, patriotic emblems and the Imperial crown.

PLATE XIV
Ribbon Rosettes
Golden Jubilee

PLATE XV
Tin Button Badges
Diamond Jubilee

PLATE XIV
Ribbon Rosettes
Golden Jubilee

Approximate value £25 each

Four ribbon rosettes with sepia photographs of Queen Victoria's family: Edward, Prince of Wales, Alexandra, Princess of Wales, young Prince Albert, Duke of Clarence and Victoria herself. These rosettes measure three and a half inches long by two and half inches wide. They were made by hand by families at home. Looped ribbon, frilled lace and gold mesh coils, trimmed with bronze motifs, were stitched to a cardboard shape, the gilt edged photographs, surmounted by a crown, would then have been glued to the centre and artificial flowers glued on around the lower edge. Simpler rosettes (see back cover) were made by pleating red, white and blue striped ribbon around a photograph of the Queen and adding ribbon streamers.

Courtesy Debrett's Peerage Ltd.

PLATE XV

Tin Button Badges
Diamond Jubilee

Approximate value £12 – £20

1. A tin button badge with Queen Victoria's head shown against a stylised Union Jack. Reverse: The Whitehead & Hoag Co., 96 & 98 Leadenhall St., London, EC, England. Made in USA.

2. A badge showing two crossed flags, the Union Jack and the Royal Standard with dates '1837 and 1897'. Reverse: Patent approved for City Button Works, USA.

3. A badge showing the young and old heads of Queen Victoria with the word 'Victoria' above together with the dates '1837 and 1898'. Reverse: The Whitehead & Hoag Co., 96 & 98 Leadenhall St., London, EC, England. Made in USA. Patent July 21, 1896. (This is a smaller version of the badge in the centre of the front cover.)

4. A badge with sepia print of Queen Victoria. Unmarked.

5. A badge with a black and white print of Queen Victoria. Unmarked.

6. A badge showing a coloured portrait of Queen Victoria. Above her head appears the legend 'Compliments of the Scottish Zoo, Glasgow, Diamond Jubilee' together with the dates '1837 and 1897'. Reverse: Whitehead & Hoag, Newark, NJ. Badges patent July 12, 1894.

7. A badge showing Queen Victoria wearing her small Imperial crown. Unmarked.

8. A floral edged badge showing a black and white portrait of Queen Victoria. Unmarked.

9. A badge showing two crossed flags, 'Diamond Jubilee' and the dates '1837 and 1897'. Unmarked.

10. A badge with a black and white print of Queen Victoria below the legend 'God save our Queen'. Reverse: The Whitehead & Hoag Co., Newark, NJ. Patented July 17, 1894, April 14, 1896, July 21, 1896.

11. A colourful badge with a portrait of Queen Victoria in front of the Union Jack and the flag of Ireland. 'Diamond Jubilee' and the dates '1837 and 1897' appear at the top. Unmarked.

Collection courtesy of Dennis Colton with the exception of number (5) Pieter Oosthuizen.

Tin button badges originated in America in the 1860s and it is there that the majority of Jubilee badges were made. The main manufacturer was 'The Whitehead & Hoag Co., in Newark, New Jersey, and around 1897 they opened branches in London and Australia. Originally made on button-making machines, the badges ranged in size from three-quarters of an inch to two and a half inches in diameter. They mainly displayed photographs of the Queen or Royal emblems and flags which were printed on to tinplate. A simple pin was attached to the back. This was done by children who undoutedly worked as outdoor workers from home. The badges were made in their thousands but as they were clearly never regarded as heirlooms, very few remain today to be collected. Queen Mary, wife of King Edward VII, collected Jubilee badges and her collection is now in the London Museum. Americans are great collectors of these badges and many must have returned to their shores. Australians are also avid collectors and they fondly refer to the badges as 'tinnies'. It is interesting to note that a fashion that began with the Diamond Jubilee is still in existence today and going from strength to strength as more and more manufacturers take to this form to advertise their goods.

PLATE XVI
Official Medals
Diamond Jubilee

1

2

PLATE XVII

Souvenir Medals
Golden and Diamond Jubilees

PLATE XVI
Official Medals
Diamond Jubilee
Approximate value £20 – £30

1. A silver medal issued to a wide range of civil and military personnel who were present on the day of the Jubilee procession or assisted in any celebration at which the Queen was present. Members of the Royal family were issued with gold medals, middle ranking civilians and Officers of the Services wore silver, and the bronze issue went to other ranks of the Army and Navy. Recipients of this medal who had also been awarded the Golden Jubilee medal could not keep both medals but rather were awarded a bar bearing the date 1897 which was fixed to the ribbon. C. Emptmeyer.

2. A bronze medal issued to all ranks of the Metropolitan Police Force who served on the day of the Jubilee procession. As with the previous medal, those men who qualified for a medal for both the Golden and Diamond Jubilees were not allowed to own two. They had to return the first one to have a simple rectangular bar with the date 1897 fitted. This medal was also awarded to members of the City of London Police Force. Unmarked.

Courtesy Ronald Hoskins.

There were well over one hundred national and local official Jubilee medals struck as well as those from Commonwealth countries and a few from non-Commonwealth countries. They were awarded to the people who officiated at either of the Jubilee processions or attended any function, at which the Queen was present, in an official capacity. Apart from the military and the Police, members of the St. John Ambulance Brigade and the Fire Brigade, present at the functions, would also be awarded a Jubilee medal. They were issued in gilt, bronze and silver and most of them were unnamed. Medals which are now inscribed would have been done so by the recipients themselves. From a collector's point of view, there is a very varied selection of official medals still to be found and the cost remains at a reasonable level.

PLATE XVII
Souvenir Medals
Golden and Diamond Jubilees
Approximate value £8 – £30

1. Silver authorised Masonic jewel with green enamelled acacia wreath, her Majesty's monogram, 'VIR', and a central medallion of Victoria, surmounted by a silver five-point star and the Imperial crown. EWS, 1887.

2. A white metal medal suspended from a gilt pin. The obverse was used for many different medals. The reverse shows the 'never setting sun' over the sea and two clasped hands. It is shown on its original card. W. O. Lewis, Birm, 1887. Reg. no. 58147.

3. Silver-gilt and paste Masonic jewel with blue and red enamel. Kenning, London, 1897.

4. A silver, diamond-shaped medal showing a profile of the Queen with her signature, 'Victoria R.I.'. The reverse shows the coat of arms for Glasgow and denotes that it was issued for a children's fête. Vaughtons, Birm, 1897.

5. A gilt medal in its original screw-top yew box, advertising a jeweller in Bishopsgate, London. Names of the colonies are entwined within a wreath on the reverse. Unmarked, 1887.

6. A copper medal of the same design as (4). Unmarked, 1897.

7. A gilt medal with blue enamelled buckled strap and red enamelled crown showing a profile of Queen Victoria with patriotic emblems around the outside. Reg. no. 57381, 1887.

8. A tiny gilt medal with red and gold ribbon. Unmarked.

9. A gilt medal, suspended from a 'souvenir' pin, with a central profile of Queen Victoria. Schwaabs & S. Co., Milwaukee, Wis., USA, 1897.

10. Silver medal with red, white and blue ribbon suspended from a silver pin. Reverse reads 'TAA'. Unmarked, 1897.

11. A gilt medal in the shape of six bells, suspended from a pin, with a faded photograph of Queen Victoria in the centre. The reverse reads, 'Canada, India, Oceana'. Reg. no. 65749, 1887.

12. A gilt medal showing some of the achievements of Victoria's reign: the bicycle, the railways, shipping and the telegraph. The reverse reads 'In commemoration of the most glorious reign on record. 1897.'

Courtesy of Les Stevens.

Souvenir medals were sometimes commissioned though mainly struck privately for commercial reasons. Businesses would use them to advertise their goods, others were used to record some particular event, and hundreds of thousands were made to be presented to school children. The Freemasons had their medals especially designed for them. Sir Albert Woods, Garter King at Arms and Grand Director of Ceremonies, designed the Golden Jubilee jewel and George Kenning & Sons designed and struck the Diamond Jubilee jewel. Most of the souvenir medals were made of base metal and extremely cheap ranging from less than a penny to the most expensive at two pounds. Far more souvenir medals were struck for the Diamond than for the Golden Jubilee; manufacturers obviously realising that this would be Victoria's last. There is still a plentiful supply of these medals for collectors to find and the best place to look, is amongst the clutter of an antiques stall.

PLATE XVIII
Primrose League Brooch
Golden Jubilee

PLATE XIX
Public Record Office Representation – Primrose League Brooch
Golden Jubilee

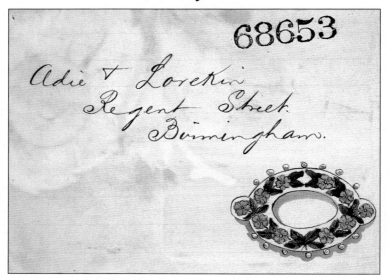

Photograph Crown copyright, Public Record Office, London.

PLATE XX
Jubilee Badge
Diamond Jubilee

PLATE XXI
Public Record Office Representation – Jubilee Badge
Diamond Jubilee

Photograph Crown copyright, Public Record Office, London.

PLATE XVIII

Primrose League Brooch
Golden Jubilee

Approximate value £100

An oval silver locket-back brooch with applied buckled strap and crown in the centre. Twisted silver wire has been soldered around the raised section in the centre and large beads have been attached around the edge. The yellow enamel flowers suggest that this brooch was made to be worn by members of the Primrose League. Reg. no. 68653.

Private collection.

The Primrose League was a political group formed in memory of Benjamin Disraeli, Lord Beaconsfield, who died in 1881. The group was formed from the Unionist and Conservative party and in 1885 a branch was founded for ladies of both the working class and the gentry. Their work was to canvass throughout the country promoting and sustaining conservative principles by interviewing people, writing letters and such like. The primrose was adopted as the emblem of the League as it was reputedly Disraeli's favourite flower and Queen Victoria, who was a great friend, would send him baskets of primroses from the woods of her home in Osborne, Isle of Wight. A range of 'Jubilee and Primrose jewellery' was launched by Keat & Co. of Goswell Road, London, where the simple primrose was combined with the Royal crown (see a second example on the front cover and advertisement on p. 41).

PLATE XIX

Public Record Office Representation – Primrose League Brooch
Golden Jubilee

A pen and ink design drawing enhanced with water colour for the 'Primrose League Brooch', reg. no. 68653.

Registered numbers replaced diamond registration marks in 1883. At the same time, five years protection to all designs on metal replaced the current three. Articles could now be sourced by looking up the registered number in the 'Registers' file at the Public Record Office in London to find the proprietor's name, address and a description of the piece. This file reveals that the brooch was registered by William Watson & Co., on 25th February, 1887. The 'Representation' file can also be looked at to find either a sketch, print or photograph.

PLATE XX
Jubilee Badge
Diamond Jubilee
Approximate value £20

A silver-gilt medal, known as the 'Jubilee badge' made to be worn as a pendant, fob hanging from a watch chain, or charm from a bracelet. Heming & Co., London. Reg. no. 296520.

Private collection.

The popular magazines of the time gave much publicity to the jewellery and trinkets that were made for the Diamond Jubilee. 'The Queen, The Lady's Newspaper', in 1897, described the 'Jubilee Badge' as '*a specially designed Jubilee badge to be worn as brooch or pendant. A really exquisite specimen of jewellers' art. In the centre is a finely executed profile of the Queen surrounded by a band bearing the names of Gt. Britain and the Colonies, and surmounted by the Imperial crown with the rose, the shamrock and the thistle on three sides. The reverse reads, "To commemorate the 60th year of the reign of H. M. Queen Victoria, 1897".*'

PLATE XXI
Public Record Office Representation – Jubilee Badge
Diamond Jubilee

A printed design, line-block and half-tone, for the 'Jubilee Badge'. The crossed-out wording suggests that the visual design of the badge only was registered and not the wording thereon. Reg. no. 296520.

For details of how to trace registered numbers, see the notes on page 38. The 'Jubilee badge' was produced by Messrs. Heming & Co., retail jewellers trading at 28 Conduit Street, London.

The Jeweller & Metalworker

Jan 1, 1887

By permission of the British Library

The Jeweller & Metalworker

Mar 15, 1887

By permission of the British Library

The Watchmaker, Jeweller & Silversmith

May 1st, 1897

By permission of the British Library

The Watchmaker, Jeweller & Silversmith

May 1st, 1897

By permission of the British Library

43

The Jubilee necklace of diamond trefoils with a pearl in
the centre of each and with a crown and pendant in the centre
presented to Queen Victoria in 1887 by the 'Women of the British Empire'.

Photograph reproduced by gracious permission of Her Majesty the Queen.

The Jubilee brooch, a pearl and diamond flower with a loop of diamonds and
a tear-drop pearl, presented to Queen Victoria in 1897
by members of her Household.

Photograph reproduced by gracious permission of Her Majesty the Queen.

Hallmarks and Makers

British hallmarking has been in existence since 1300. It acts as a safeguard to anyone buying an article of precious metal as the hallmark acts as a guarantee of purity. However, in the case of jewellery, pieces under 7.8 grams in weight were exempt from hallmarking which makes authenticating them difficult.

Hallmarks, or assay marks, consist of three symbols: the office mark, the standard mark and the date letter. From these three marks one can determine where the article was registered, who manufactured it and at what date. The office mark tells us whether the article was assayed in Birmingham (anchor), Chester (shield bearing the arms of the City) or London (leopard's head). The standard mark of British silver is the lion passant which indicates that the silver is of 92.5 parts silver to 7.5 parts copper. The date letter is a different letter of the alphabet each year, in alphabetical order, and when repeated, distinguished from the others by a different style. Hallmarks on gold are the same as silver except that instead of a lion passant, nine carat gold bears the number .375, eighteen carat has the number 18 and a crown, and twenty-two carat has the number 22 and a crown.

When dating a piece of Jubilee jewellery it must be remembered that the date letter was changed annually in the month of July. This explains why there is sometimes a discrepancy in that an '1897' motif may appear on the front of the piece whereas the date letter could be 1896.

As well as assay marks, most silver and gold jewellery bears a maker's or sponsor's mark which consists of a set of initials enclosed within a frame.

Maker's marks on Jubilee jewellery are very difficult to source. There can be as many as twenty-six makers with the same initials and although the frame around the initials should vary with each maker, it is often difficult to define. It is only when a mark is particularly distinctive, or when we find further references, that we can be sure of the maker. Prolific manufacturers, such as Sydenham Bros. (S. Bros.), Joseph William Tonks (J.W.T.), or Pepper, Payton & Co., (PP & Co.), can be identified with certainty. These manufacturers can be found amongst the trade advertisements of the time in The Watchmaker, Jeweller and Silversmith and The Jeweller and Metalworker. To confuse things further, a London silversmith may have had a piece assayed in Birmingham. Another point to remember is that a design may be registered by a proprietor who might be an agent, wholesaler or retailer, and not necessarily the manufacturer.

Sydenham Bros.
Birmingham
1896

Jubilee Jewellery on cover

Reading from left to right downwards with cover open

1. Three silver threepenny pieces soldered together. Unmarked. 1887.
2. Red, white and blue ribbon rosette with photograph of Queen Victoria by Bassano. Unmarked.
3. Tin badge with sepia photograph of Queen Victoria. Unmarked.
4. A silver, circular, beaded-edge brooch with an enamelled Royal Standard. Unmarked. 1887.
5. Base metal 'Victoria' brooch. Unmarked. 1887.
6. A silver bar brooch with crown and 'VR' applied. A & LLd, Birm, 1896.
7. A Primrose League circular, scalloped-edge brooch with applied crown and enamelled primrose. Unmarked. 1887.
8. A hollow silver brooch with young and old heads of the Queen surmounted by a crown. Reg. no. 280776. T.S.B., Chester, 1897.
9. A brass badge with red, white and blue enamel and the date 1897. Unmarked.
10. A silver charm with the old head of Queen Victoria. Unmarked.
11. A celluloid button badge with gilt frame. City Button Works, New York, 1897.
12. A crescent-shaped, beaded-edge brooch surmounted by a crown. H & L, Birm, 1896.
13. A tiny silver charm, 1897. Reg. no. 292118. Unmarked.
14. An oblong silver, beaded-edge brooch with turquoise enamel flag, red 'V' and 'R' and enamelled Royal Standard. 1887. Unmarked.
15. Tin button badge with young and old head of Victoria. Whitehead & Hoag Co., 96 & 98 Leadenhall St., London, EC, England. Made in USA. Patent July 21, 1896. Photo courtesy of Museum of London.
16. A hollow silver profile of Queen Victoria wearing her Imperial crown. C & N, Birm, 1896.
17. A brass quatrefoil medal with red and blue enamel, 1897. Unmarked.
18. A circular, scalloped-edge brooch with applied crown and young head of Victoria. Marked 'sterling silver'.
19. Gold coloured tin button badge with flags of England and Ireland. 1897. Unmarked.
20. A silver crown-shaped brooch with crossed flags and an enamelled Royal Standard. Unmarked.
21. A young profile of Victoria surmounted on a bar brooch with 'V' and 'R' applied and 'Jubilee' engraved. Marked 'fine silver'.
22. White enamelled base metal 'Pass, no. 500'. Bowman Ltd., Goswell Road, London, 1897.
23. An oval, silver beaded-edge brooch with applied crown and patriotic emblems. J. E., Birm, 1896.
24. A brass plaque of Victoria. Reverse reads, 'Serjeant's Stores, 181 Newington Butts, SE.' 1887.
25. A brass medal, Golden Jubilee. Unmarked.
26. A brass Diamond Jubilee medal with sepia photograph of Queen Victoria and a fragment of red, white and blue ribbon. Unmarked.
27. An oval, scalloped silver brooch with 'V' and 'R', a crown and a shield applied. Unmarked.
28. An enamelled mace with an applied crescent-shaped, beaded-edge, motif enclosing two enamelled shields. Unmarked.
29. A base metal brooch with red and blue enamel and inscription, 'Queen and Empress, 1837 – 1897'. Unmarked.

Photographer: Peter White, FXP Photography